THE
LITTLE LOCAL
TEXAS
COOKBOOK

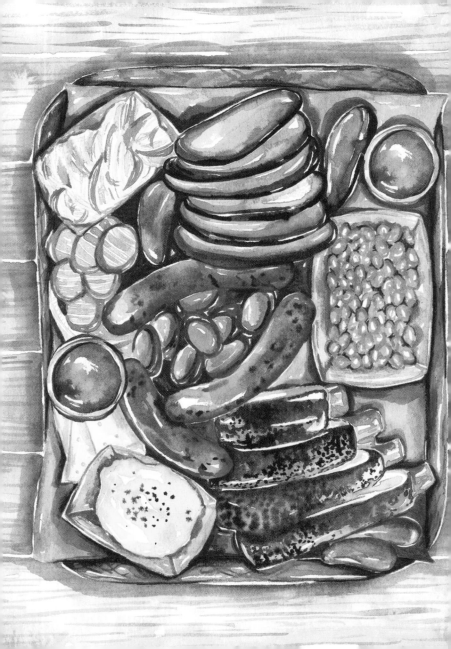

THE
LITTLE LOCAL
TEXAS
COOKBOOK

Recipes for Classic Dishes

HILAH JOHNSON

THE COUNTRYMAN PRESS
A division of W. W. Norton & Company
Independent Publishers Since 1923

For information about permission to reproduce selections from this
book, write to Permissions, The Countryman Press, 500 Fifth Avenue,
New York, NY 10110

For information about special discounts for bulk purchases, please
contact W. W. Norton Special Sales at
specialsales@wwnorton.com or 800-233-4830

Manufacturing by Versa Press
Book design by Debbie Berne
Production manager: Devon Zahn

Library of Congress Cataloging-in-Publication Data

Names: Johnson, Hilah, author.
Title: The little local Texas cookbook / Hilah Johnson.
Description: New York, NY : W. W. Norton & Company, Inc., [2019] |
    Includes index.
Identifiers: LCCN 2019006203 | ISBN 9781682684191 (hardcover)
Subjects: LCSH: Cooking—Texas. | Cooking, American. | LCGFT:
    Cookbooks.
Classification: LCC TX714 .J622 2019 | DDC 641.59764—dc23
LC record available at https://lccn.loc.gov/2019006203

The Countryman Press
www.countrymanpress.com

A division of W. W. Norton & Company, Inc.
500 Fifth Avenue, New York, NY 10110
www.wwnorton.com

978-1-68268-419-1

10 9 8 7 6 5 4 3 2 1

For Flint

CONTENTS

Sides

Breakfast and Brunch

Desserts

INTRODUCTION

Three-meat barbecue plates with unlimited pickles, onions, and soft white bread. Cheese enchilada platters. Crisp, breaded, chicken-fried steaks, ladled with white cream gravy. Backyard fish fries and community chili cook-offs. Chips and queso. Crunchy beef tacos. Pillowy soft kolaches. Pecan pie. These are some of the finest foods Texas has to offer.

While many classics, including chili, chicken-fried steak, and queso, are found the whole state over, other famous Texas dishes are regional. Dry-rubbed barbecue brisket is still mostly found in central Texas, and breakfast tacos aren't seen much north of Dallas. Kolache bakeries nestle inside the "Texas Triangle," formed by connecting the dots of Dallas, Houston, and San Antonio. The freshest fried fish can be found at shacks in east Texas and down the Gulf Coast. The Rio Grande Valley's got the best flour tortillas you'll ever eat in your life. Depending on the region, wild foods such as Mustang grapes, *chile pequin* peppers, and prickly pear cactus, are still featured in home kitchens.

Texas cuisine has been influenced by Mexican and African-American cuisines, giving rise respectively to two of our most famous exports: Tex-Mex and barbecue. It's also been influenced by Native American, Cajun, Creole, British, Irish, German, Czech, Chinese, Vietnamese, Italian, Jewish, and Dutch cuisines, among many others. The Spanish conquistadors brought rice and pigs. Native Americans shared the science of *nixtamalization*—the process of turning corn into hominy and then into masa and tortillas.

Tex-Mex developed out of northern Mexican cuisine, incorporating ingredients such as fresh, dried, and pickled chiles; tortillas; and beans; and adding more dairy, beef, wheat, and cumin. The Queso (page 14), Texas Chili (page 25), Fajitas (page 36), Crispy Tacos (page 48), Breakfast Tacos (page 64), and Tex-Mex Cheese Enchiladas (page 40) recipes in this book are quintessential Tex-Mex—and can all contribute to the wondrous concept of the "combo plate." A Tex-Mex combo plate usually includes an enchilada, a crispy taco, and more rice and beans than you probably can eat.

Brought to Texas by African Americans, barbecue is a vastly important part of the state's history and culture; producing good barbecue in your own

backyard is a badge of honor. Beef brisket and ribs are what most people think of as "Texas-style barbecue," but while beef barbecue is popular now, it wasn't until after the Civil War and the cattle drives that followed that Texas became synonymous with beef. Before that, pork was the most commonly eaten meat in the state. Sauced and chopped, East-Texas-style barbecue pork, a descendent of Carolina-style barbecue, is considered by many historians to be the true original Texas barbecue.

Chicken-Fried Steak (page 32) was born from traditional Wiener schnitzel recipes brought by German immigrants. It quickly adapted to life in Texas by being remade with tenderized beef steak and obliterated by cream gravy. Czechs also came to Texas, bringing with them their fruit-filled Kolaches (page 68). Within a generation, bakers were stuffing cheese and sausage inside them instead. Of course, like everywhere, there's a continuous push-pull of cultures in the kitchen, but it does seem like "more dairy, more beef" is a constant you can always count on in Texas.

In this book, you'll find all these recipes and more, along with their deeper histories, because somewhere between its food and history lies the heart of a place.

Welcome to Texas.

APPETIZERS
AND
DRINKS

QUESO

Makes 12 servings

Chips and queso are the quintessential Texas appetizer, because nothing says "Tex-Mex" like buckets of dairy products and cheese. The queen of cheese has got to be Velveeta, and it's the only cheese that'll do when it's time to make queso. (Word to the wise: refrigerate leftover queso and use it as a sandwich spread, or add it to some scrambled eggs to make the best breakfast tacos ever. It will keep for a week or more in the refrigerator.)

1 large onion, finely diced

2 tablespoons bacon fat, butter, or margarine

2 10-ounce cans diced tomatoes with green chiles (look for Ro-Tel brand)

1 2-pound block Velveeta cheese, sliced into 1-inch chunks

Diced avocado, chopped cilantro, and sliced green onions for topping, optional

Tortilla chips for serving

In a large skillet over medium-high heat, sauté the onion in the bacon fat until soft and translucent, about 5 minutes. Stir in the tomatoes with chiles and their juices and then the cheese. Reduce the heat to low and cook, stirring frequently, until smooth and melted, about 8 minutes. Gently fold in the toppings, if using. Serve right away with the tortilla chips.

Note: If serving for a party, it's easiest to transfer queso to a slow cooker on low heat for holding. If your slow cooker doesn't have a removable insert, save yourself a lot of trouble and put your queso in a glass or metal bowl that fits inside the cooker and can rest on the lip. Fill the slow cooker halfway with water and use it as a double boiler.

Note: For an even simpler version, omit the onion and bacon fat. Combine cubed Velveeta with canned tomatoes and peppers in a microwave-safe bowl and microwave on high, stirring every 90 seconds, until melted and smooth, about 5 minutes.

. . .

NACHOS

Makes 2 to 4 servings

Nachos were invented by a clever maître d'hôtel in the border city of Piedras Negras, Mexico, in the 1940s. When a group of hungry Americans arrived after the kitchen was closed, Ignacio "Nacho" Anaya put together a simple snack that became a fantastic hit. The original recipe was topped with only grated cheese and pickled jalapeño peppers, but many Texans also add refried beans and garnish their nachos with sour cream and guacamole. Use a standard or thick-cut tortilla chip here, rather than a thin and crispy variety. Nachos make a hearty appetizer for four or—true to their origin—an easy and quick late-night dinner for two.

Continued

1 13-ounce bag tortilla chips

1 cup refried pinto beans

1½ cups grated cheese
(mild Cheddar, Monterey
Jack, or a Mexican blend)

⅓ cup pickled jalapeño
slices, drained

4 green onions, thinly sliced;
¼ cup sour cream; and ½ batch
Guacamole (see below) for topping

1 Heat the oven to 350°F and place a rack in the middle of the oven.

2 Get out a large baking sheet. Spread 1 teaspoon or so of refried beans on each chip. Take your time: perfect nachos benefit from a little patience. Use only the biggest chips and those that are whole (tip: save your broken chips for Chicken Tortilla Soup, page 42, or Migas, page 68).

3 Arrange the chips in a layer on the baking sheet, overlapping them slightly. Sprinkle evenly with the cheese. Dot with the jalapeño slices. Bake until the cheese is melted, 5 to 8 minutes.

4 Remove from the oven and serve as is, or top with the green onions, sour cream, and Guacamole.

· · ·

GUACAMOLE

Makes 6 servings (1½ cups)

The name guacamole comes from the Aztec *āhuacamolli*, literally "avocado sauce," and at its simplest, the dish is just avocado mashed with salt. Serve it with tortilla chips (or jicama sticks if you're on a no-chip diet) or use it to top nachos, fajitas, or even a burger. Guacamole is best eaten within a few hours of making it. Don't bother saving the pit to put on top; the lime juice is what keeps the guacamole bright green.

2 Hass avocados	¼ cup minced fresh cilantro
Freshly squeezed juice of 1 lime (about 2 tablespoons), plus more as needed	2 tablespoons minced green onion or shallot
	1 clove garlic, minced
1 jalapeño pepper or serrano chile, minced (seeds and membranes removed for less heat)	½ teaspoon salt

1 Hold the avocado in your palm. Using a sharp knife, cut around it longitudinally to create two symmetrical halves. Twist the halves apart and use your knife to remove the pit. Squeeze the avocado flesh out into a bowl and sprinkle the lime juice all over it.

2 Mash up the avocado with a fork to your preferred smoothness. Stir in everything else.

3 Taste and add some more lime juice or salt if you think it needs it. Serve right away or cover tightly and refrigerate up to 2 hours.

Note: A ripe Hass avocado should be dark green to black in color and should yield slightly when pressed near the stem end. If you have the foresight to do so, it's best to buy them when they're firm and green and place them in a paper bag to ripen at home in 4 to 5 days. Avocados that feel ripe at the store are often bruised inside.

TEXAS CAVIAR

Makes 4 servings (2 cups)

Like Southerners, Texans eat black-eyed peas on New Year's Day for good luck. Supposedly, for each pea you eat on January 1, you'll get a day of good luck in the new year. You can stew your black-eyed peas with tomatoes and onions, but Texas Caviar is another option, and it's not just for the new year—this is a popular potluck dish all year round. Serve it as a chunky dip or as a side dish. It keeps very well in the fridge for several days and it's easy to double the recipe for a crowd.

1 15-ounce can unseasoned black-eyed peas, drained and rinsed

3 tablespoons canola oil or mild olive oil

1 tablespoon apple cider vinegar or red wine vinegar

1 bunch green onions, thinly sliced (about 1 cup)

¼ cup diced red bell pepper

1 jalapeño pepper, minced

1 clove garlic, minced

¼ teaspoon salt

¼ teaspoon cayenne pepper or sweet paprika

Tortilla chips or Fritos for serving, optional

Combine all the ingredients in a bowl. Refrigerate at least 1 hour before serving as a dip with chips or as a side dish.

CLASSIC MARGARITA

Makes one 3-ounce cocktail

A good margarita just needs three ingredients: tequila (I like silver, but if you like añejo tequilas, go for it), lime juice, and orange liqueur. A ratio of 3:2:1 is my preference for flavor. It's also easy to remember, which is important when you are knee-deep in Margaritaville. For the salt, just use coarse kosher salt; there's no need to pay extra for "margarita salt." This classic margarita is bright and tangy, and not too sweet.

1 lime wedge	1½ ounces tequila
Coarse kosher salt	1 ounce lime juice
Ice	½ ounce Cointreau or triple sec

1 If you like salt, rub the lime wedge around the rim of an 8-ounce tumbler glass to get it damp. Spread some salt out in a small saucer and dip the lip of the glass in it. Tap off the excess. Fill the glass with ice.

2 Fill a shaker with more ice and add the tequila, lime juice, and liqueur. Shake well and strain into the glass. Garnish with the lime wedge.

Note: If you're into spicy drinks, muddle several slices of serrano chile or habanero pepper in the shaker before adding the liquids.

MEXICAN MARTINI

Makes one 6-ounce cocktail

I first had this drink in Austin. It's like a margarita, but with the addition of orange juice, Sprite, and . . . olive juice? Garnishing this drink with olives (preferably jalapeño-stuffed ones) may sound weird, but thinking of the olives as a replacement for the salted rim of a classic margarita helps it all make sense.

Ice

2 ounces silver tequila

1 ounce triple sec

1 ounce orange juice

1 ounce lime juice

1 ounce Sprite

Garnish: large green olives on a pick

Fill a shaker with ice and add the tequila, triple sec, orange and lime juices, and Sprite. Shake well and strain into a martini glass, garnished with the olives. Each person gets his or her own glass and shaker jar to refill as needed.

ICED TEA

Makes 1 quart

This section wouldn't be complete without a mention of iced tea. It's an all-day drink for many Texans, and it's served unsweetened— perhaps with a lemon wedge or a sprig of mint, but if you want it sweet, you'll have to do it yourself. Most people I know enjoy it without sugar and for reasons not proven by science, iced tea is infinitely more hydrating than water. It's also the best hangover cure I know. So while you're mixing up margaritas, steep a pitcher of tea for the fridge, too. You'll thank yourself the next day.

6 black tea bags	Lemon wedges (optional)
2 cups ice cubes	Mint leaves (optional)

Place 6 black tea bags in a heat-proof pitcher (I use a four-cup Pyrex measuring cup), add 2 cups boiling water, and let steep 5 minutes. Remove and discard the tea bags; add sweetener now if you like. Stir in 2 cups of ice cubes until melted, and then refrigerate. Serve over more ice with lemon wedges and/or mint leaves.

MAINS

TEXAS CHILI
(and Frito Pie!)

Makes 8 servings

As chili is the official state food of Texas, a good recipe for it is an absolute must in any Texan's kitchen repertoire. This one comes from my daddy, who learned to make it from his granddaddy. The thing that makes a proper Texas chili isn't so much what goes in it, but what doesn't. And that's beans. Ain't no beans in a Texas chili—just meat, chili powder, onion, and tomatoes. Chili really gained its foothold in Texas during the 1930s via the Chili Queens of San Antonio, who sold chili in the plazas by the bowlful. Some people like their chili made with ground beef, and others use stew meat chunks. I like an in-between texture achieved by using a coarse-ground beef called "chili grind." Try venison, too, if you're lucky enough to get some. Use pure ancho chile powder if you can find it. Many "chili powder" brands are actually blended with salt and other spices, and while they will work in this recipe, you may need to reduce the additional salt. Cornbread (page 60) makes a perfect accompaniment.

2 pounds coarse-ground chuck roast

1 very large onion, finely diced

2 to 5 jalapeño peppers, minced

6 cloves garlic, minced
(2 tablespoons)

¼ cup ancho chile powder

2 tablespoons ground cumin

1 tablespoon sweet paprika

1 teaspoon dried oregano

Continued

1 teaspoon cayenne pepper,
optional for extra spicy chili

1 28-ounce can diced tomatoes

1 12-ounce can beer

1½ teaspoons salt

1 corn tortilla, torn into pieces,
optional for thickening

1 Place the beef in a large pot over medium-high heat and break it up with a large spoon (there should be enough fat that you don't need to add any oil). Add the onion, jalapeños, garlic, and spices. Fry until the onions start to soften and the spices are toasted.

2 Reduce the heat to medium and add the tomatoes, beer, and salt. Bring to a simmer.

3 Reduce the heat to low, cover, and simmer, stirring occasionally, 2 hours.

4 Taste and add more salt if it needs it. If you'd like it thicker, stir in the corn tortilla pieces and simmer another 30 minutes. Chili tastes better the day after making it and keeps in the fridge at least 1 week.

Note: Most of the alcohol from the beer will cook off, but not all of it. You may use chicken or beef stock in place of the beer.

• • •

FRITO PIE

All you need to do to make a Frito Pie is put a few handfuls of Fritos in a bowl and top with a cup of chili, some shredded Cheddar, a few pickled jalapeño slices, and some diced white onion. Sprinkle a few more Fritos on top and eat. If you can find single-serving bags of Fritos, do what we used to do as kids: split open the side of the bag, put it on a plate and make the Frito pie right in the bag. No dirty bowl!

SMOKED BRISKET

*Makes varies, but allow ½ pound of raw
starting weight per person*

Texas is probably known best for its barbecue—specifically, beef brisket. Although east-Texas barbecue is still quite pork-heavy and south Texas serves a lot of barbacoa, the central-Texas style of dry-rubbed beef with no sauce has become the style that most people associate with Texas. If you're practiced and comfortable using a smoker, try barbecuing a brisket. If you've never used a smoker before, I strongly recommend starting off with my oven method and practicing smoking some easier meats first, like pork butt or chicken quarters. Plan to cook a brisket for 1½ hours per pound of beef (that's 18 hours for a 12-pound brisket!), but brisket is notoriously finicky and the cooking time can be hours longer than what the math said. Smoked or roasted, start a couple of hours earlier than you think you should. To hold a hot brisket until guests arrive, line a beer cooler with towels and place the foil-wrapped, cooked brisket inside; it will hold nice and hot for 3 hours. And of course, nowadays every joint in town has its own house-made barbecue sauce, but the tradition is that barbecue brisket should stand on its own without needing the extra moisture or flavor of a sauce. Beer, Iced Tea (page 21), Charro Beans (page 52), Potato Salad (page 56), Coleslaw (page 58), white bread, flour tortillas, pickles, onions, and hot sauce most certainly do belong on the table, though. (Watch yourself, son! That hot

Continued

sauce is for the beans only! Just kidding—you can put a little on your brisket, too, if you want to.)

1 whole 8- to 12-pound beef brisket	1 teaspoon dry mustard powder
2 tablespoons freshly ground black pepper	For smoked brisket: 8 ounces hardwood chunks (oak, mesquite, pecan)
2 to 3 teaspoons coarse kosher salt	
1 teaspoon onion powder	For oven brisket: 1 teaspoon smoked paprika

1 Trim the brisket. An untrimmed brisket will have a thick "fat cap" over one side, sometimes up to 1 inch or more. Use a sharp, flexible knife to shave it to about ⅓ inch. Too much fat will flame up in your smoker, and too little will make a dry brisket.

2 Combine the rub ingredients in a small bowl and coat evenly: top, bottom, and all around. Refrigerate up to 24 hours if you want to.

3 If you have an oven-safe meat thermometer, put it into the thickest part of the brisket before you start cooking. A remote thermometer is best so you can watch the temperature without opening the smoker. You'll need to keep an eye on the smoker or oven temperature, and also the interior meat temperature.

To smoke:

1 Get your smoker going and stabilize the temperature around 230°F. Add a couple of handfuls of wood chunks to the coals and place the seasoned brisket on the rack. Close the smoker. Maintain the smoker temperature to between 225°F to 235°F and keep the smoke looking thin and blue. When the smoke slows, add another handful of wood chunks. Do this for the first 2 hours. After 4 or so hours, the brisket's internal temperature may plateau somewhere between 150°F to 170°F.

2 That's when you want the "Texas Crutch": wrap the brisket tightly in heavy-duty aluminum foil and put it back in the smoker until the internal temperature reaches about 195°F. This may take 10 to 12 hours more. Once the temperature is up around 195°F, unwrap it and give it the jiggle test. If it's floppy, like Jell-O, or a skewer goes in with no resistance, it's ready. If it's not, let it go longer. The exact time it takes is unpredictable, and it's better to have brisket waiting on guests than vice versa. So always start a couple of hours earlier than you think you should, and if you need to hold the brisket, get out the towel-lined beer cooler. When you're ready to serve, allow the brisket to rest on a cutting board at room temperature for 30 minutes before unwrapping, slicing against the grain, and serving.

To roast:

Heat the oven to 250°F and get out a roasting pan big enough to hold the brisket. Put a rack in the bottom. No rack? Line the pan with thick onion slices. Put the brisket on the rack, fat side up. Cover tightly with foil and roast 12 to 16 hours, depending on the size. Don't mess with it. When the internal temperature reaches between 195°F and 205°F and/or the brisket easily jiggles when you move it around, it's ready. Always go by feel over time and temperature. Once it's jiggly, remove the foil and bake another 30 minutes to get a semblance of "bark" on it. Remove from the oven, cover loosely, and let rest 30 minutes before slicing against the grain and serving.

BEEF BACK RIBS

Makes 3 to 4 servings

While producing a great barbecue brisket is considered the pinnacle for any Pit Master, beginners will find smoked beef ribs a lot easier and still delicious. Where brisket can take an untold amount of time, beef back ribs are typically done in under 6 hours. Where brisket requires careful attention to slicing against the grain, beef ribs just require a hand to hold them and teeth to bite, like giant corn-on-the-cobs for carnivores. Beef back ribs aren't commonly found at butchers, so you may have to special order them. Allow one rib per person and serve with the same accoutrement as a brisket plate.

1 3- to 4-pound rack beef back ribs

1 tablespoon coarsely ground black pepper

1 teaspoon salt

½ teaspoon dry mustard

4 ounces hardwood chunks

Remove the silverskin from the ribs. Combine the dry rub ingredients in a small bowl and rub it in all over the meat and bones.

To smoke:

Get your smoker going and stabilize the temperature around 230°F. Add a couple of handfuls of wood chunks and place the ribs on the rack. Close the smoker. Maintain the smoker temperature to between 225°F to 235°F and keep the smoke looking thin and blue. When the smoke slows, add another handful of wood chunks. The ribs are ready when the meat is easily pierced with a skewer and just beginning to pull away from the bone.

To roast:

Heat the oven to 250°F and get out a roasting pan big enough to hold the ribs. If you have a rack, put that in there too. Put the ribs on the rack, meat side up. Cover tightly with foil and roast 4 hours. No peeking! Ribs are done when the meat is very tender and the bones have just begun to release from the meat. Uncover and pop the pan under the broiler for just 1 minute to brown them a little. Cool 10 minutes before slicing between the ribs and serving.

CHICKEN-FRIED STEAK

Makes 4 servings

If you've never heard of Chicken-Fried Steak, you might think there's chicken in it, but instead it's cube steak that is breaded and fried as you would chicken. I'm lucky that my dad taught me how to make the best chicken-fried steak on the planet, and now I'm teaching you. The thing that makes this the best is its cracker-crumb coating. It's nontraditional, but once you try it this way, you won't go back to plain ol' flour breading ever again—unless someday the earth runs out of crackers and if that happens, we'll have bigger problems anyway, I bet. On timing this meal, I usually boil my potatoes first and hold them in the hot water, heat off, until my steaks and gravy are done. Hold the steaks on low heat while you drain and mash the potatoes real quick. Of course, you don't have to serve this with mashed potatoes, but Texans are always looking for more things to put cream gravy on, so we do.

1 pound thin-cut cube steak or round steak

½ teaspoon salt

2 whole large eggs

½ cup all-purpose flour

1 teaspoon freshly ground black pepper

½ sleeve saltine crackers, crushed into about 2 cups crumbs

¼ cup vegetable oil or bacon fat or a combination of the two

Gravy (page 70)

1 Heat the oven to 200°F. Lay the steak on a cutting board and gently pound with the flat side of a meat mallet, working from the center toward the edges until about 1/3 inch thick. Sprinkle with salt on each side and go over each one again with the pokey side of the mallet. Be gentle. Don't tear the meat. Cut it into 4 portions.

2 Beat the eggs well in a shallow bowl. Mix the flour with the black pepper in a separate shallow bowl. Crush the crackers and put them on a plate. Now dip each steak in this order: egg, flour, egg, crackers. Set the steak aside. (Once finished breading, you can lightly cover with wax paper and refrigerate several hours before cooking.)

3 Warm half the oil in a large skillet over high heat. When the oil is hot enough, a fleck of cracker crumb will sizzle when tossed in. Cook the steaks about 3 minutes, and then turn over and reduce the heat to medium-high. Add more oil if needed and cook until just barely pink in the middle, about 4 minutes more. Fry the steaks without crowding them, even if you have to do one at a time. If you cram too much in the skillet, they will steam instead of fry, and your breading will come off.

4 Remove from the heat and keep the steaks warm on a sheet in the oven. Plate and serve with gravy.

Note: I have known people (Texans, even!) who serve CFS with ketchup instead of gravy. While I can't sanction that blasphemy myself, go on and do it if you want to. You will probably still get into Heaven.

FRIED FISH

Makes 4 to 6 servings

Anyone who grew up near the Gulf Coast knows all about fried fish, as does anyone who grew up near one of Texas's lakes or rivers. This cornmeal breading makes quick work of catfish, trout, and redfish, but try it with any firm white fish fillets that are no thicker than ¾ inch. When I was a kid growing up on Lake Travis, we always ate our fried catfish with gobs of bottled tartar sauce. Nowadays, I wrap fried fish in hot corn tortillas and top it with a lime–cilantro slaw, making fish tacos. Either way you serve it, Peach Cobbler (page 74) makes a fine dessert.

FOR THE FISH

1 pound thin fish fillets, skinned or scaled

1 cup buttermilk

1 tablespoon minced fresh parsley

¼ teaspoon salt

Few dashes Tabasco sauce or to taste

FOR THE BREADING

1 cup cornmeal

1 tablespoon cornstarch

¼ teaspoon cayenne pepper

¼ teaspoon freshly ground black pepper

¼ teaspoon salt

About 3 cups oil for frying

1 Cut the fish into pieces about 1 inch wide by about 4 inches long. In a bowl, combine the buttermilk, parsley, salt, and Tabasco and immerse the fish in the marinade. Allow to sit at room temperature 10 to 20 minutes. Drain well.

2 Combine the cornmeal, cornstarch, cayenne pepper, black pepper, and salt in a shallow bowl. Coat each piece of fish in the breading and set aside on a rack to rest while the oil reaches temperature.

3 Heat ½ inch of oil in a deep skillet to 360 to 365°F. Fry a few pieces at a time (don't overcrowd the skillet) for about 2 minutes on each side, or until they float up from the bottom of the skillet. Remove to a rack over paper towels to drain for at least 3 minutes. Repeat until all the fish has been fried.

4 Serve warm.

FAJITAS

Makes 8 servings (16 tacos)

Fajitas are grilled beef flank or skirt steak that's sliced real thin, and wrapped in hot tortillas with grilled peppers and onions. The word *fajitas* means "little strips." Although chicken, shrimp, and even pork fajitas are commonplace now, if I picked one that exemplified Texas cookouts, it's beef fajitas. If you'd rather not mess around with a charcoal grill, you can cook the meat on a big, hot griddle and roast the vegetables in the oven.

2 bell or poblano peppers, kept whole

2 yellow or white onions, halved lengthwise

Vegetable oil

1 teaspoon salt, plus more for seasoning

¼ cup freshly squeezed lime juice

¼ cup Worcestershire sauce

2 tablespoons minced garlic

1 teaspoon salt

½ teaspoon freshly ground black pepper

2 pounds flank or skirt steak (no thicker than 1 inch)

16 to 18 flour or corn tortillas (see Note), salsa of your choice, sour cream or Mexican crema, Guacamole (page 16), grated cheese (Cheddar, Monterey Jack, Manchego), and pico de gallo (see Note) for serving

1   Rub the peppers and onion halves with oil and sprinkle with a little salt. In a large bowl, stir together the lime juice, Worcestershire sauce, garlic, 1 teaspoon salt, and black pepper and put the meat in the marinade. Cover and marinate at room temperature for 1 hour or refrigerate for a few hours.

2 In the meantime, get your charcoal grill started. Pile up the coals in the center and light them on fire. Cover the grill and let it burn until the temperature is about 450°F. Once the coals are covered in white ash and the grill is hot, spread the coals out a little bit.

3 Lay the meat out in a single layer. You may have to do 2 batches. Place the peppers and onions around the outside of the grill to roast. Grill the meat, uncovered, for 2 to 4 minutes on each side, depending on thickness. Turn the peppers and onions as needed to cook evenly, but you do want to get some good char on them.

4 When the meat is done, transfer to a cutting board to rest a few minutes. If the vegetables need more time, move them to a hotter part of the grill while the meat rests. Slice the meat against the grain and slice up the roasted peppers and onions. Warm some tortillas on the grill (or just in the microwave) and set out the salsa, sour cream, Guacamole, grated cheese, and pico de gallo. Allow guests to assemble their own fajitas.

Note: While I prefer corn tortillas for other types of tacos, when it comes to beef fajitas and breakfast tacos, I always opt for flour.

Note: Pico de gallo is a very easy salsa to make. Just combine 1 cup diced tomato, ½ cup diced onion, ¼ cup minced cilantro, 1 minced jalapeño pepper, and lime juice, minced garlic, and salt to taste.

SERRANO CHEESEBURGERS

Makes 4 servings

There's a bar in Austin called Casino El Camino that is famous for their Amarillo Burger laden with grilled serrano chiles, Pepper Jack cheese, and cilantro mayo, and this is my home-made version of that burger. It's guaranteed to knock some sense into you. Beware when handling serrano chiles—if you have sensitive skin, wear food-safe gloves or handle the peppers with tongs to avoid contact with your skin. And wash up well with soap afterward!

FOR THE CILANTRO MAYONNAISE

¼ cup mayonnaise

2 tablespoons minced fresh cilantro

1 small clove garlic, minced

FOR THE BURGERS

4 serrano chiles

1½ pounds ground chuck (80% lean)

1 teaspoon salt

1 teaspoon freshly ground black pepper

4 thick slices Pepper Jack

8 leaves crisp iceberg lettuce

4 hamburger buns

Yellow mustard, optional

Make the cilantro mayonnaise:

Combine all the mayonnaise ingredients and mix well. Refrigerate.

Make the burgers:

1 Heat the oven to broil.

2 Broil the serrano chiles until roasted and blackened, 1 minute or so on each side. Remove from the oven and let cool (leave the oven on). Coarsely chop the chiles, discarding the stems.

3 Form the meat into four thin patties, no thicker than a half-inch. Make the centers a little thinner than the edges.

4 Heat a large, heavy (cast-iron preferred) skillet or griddle over medium-high heat. Sprinkle the burger patties with salt and black pepper just before placing in the hot skillet. Cook for 3 to 6 minutes per side, depending on how you like your burgers. Add cheese slices and remove from the heat.

5 Toast the buns in the broiler and then slather 1 side of each with cilantro mayo. Top with a cheesy burger patty, some chopped roasted serrano chiles, and lettuce. Spread more cilantro mayo and/or yellow mustard on the top bun to hold it all together.

TEX-MEX CHEESE ENCHILADAS

Makes 4 to 6 servings (12 enchiladas)

Cheese enchiladas were one of my favorite foods as a kid, and they still are today. My dad made them with grated yellow Cheddar, corn tortillas, diced white onion, and a can of enchilada sauce. While canned enchilada sauce is a great invention, making your own from scratch is pretty easy. For a vegetarian twist (which is really just as good), omit the beef and sauté the onion in 1 teaspoon of vegetable oil instead; substitute vegetable broth for the chicken stock.

¼ pound ground beef

1 medium onion, diced

3 tablespoons bacon fat or vegetable oil

3 tablespoons all-purpose flour

2 tablespoons tomato paste

2 tablespoons chili powder

1 teaspoon dried oregano

1 teaspoon salt

½ teaspoon ground cumin

½ teaspoon freshly ground black pepper

2 cups chicken or beef stock

12 corn tortillas

1 tablespoon vegetable oil for warming tortillas

6 ounces grated Cheddar or Colby Jack (about 1½ cups)

Thinly sliced green onions and cooked rice and beans for serving

1 Heat the oven to 350°F (or use the microwave).

2 In a large skillet over medium heat, brown the meat with ½ the diced onion, breaking up the meat into very small pieces. Once fully cooked, transfer to a bowl and set aside.

3 Add the oil to the skillet and place over medium heat until it's very warm. Add the flour and whisk to combine. Let cook, stirring constantly, until the color darkens and it starts to smell toasted, about 2 minutes. Add the tomato paste and the spices. The mixture will thicken up immediately, but continue stirring it until smooth. Whisk in ½ the stock and mix until smooth. Add the remaining stock and the cooked beef and onion. Cover and simmer 5 minutes.

4 Meanwhile, warm the tortillas on an oiled griddle until pliable. Mix the cheese and remaining diced onion together. Roll about 2 tablespoons of the cheese mixture into each tortilla and pack them tightly into a 9-by-13-inch pan (usually you'll have to line 10 up the long side of the pan and then slide 2 in lengthwise).

5 Spread sauce to cover the enchiladas. Sprinkle any remaining cheese and onion on top. Bake until cheese is melted, about 15 minutes, or microwave on high about 5 minutes. Serve sprinkled with the green onions, rice, and beans.

CHICKEN TORTILLA SOUP

Makes 4 servings

You'll find Chicken Tortilla Soup (often just called Tortilla Soup) on pretty much every menu in Texas, and almost every household has its own stand-by recipe. It's a rich chicken soup seasoned with chiles and tomatoes, enriched with the nuttiness of corn tortillas, and served with crunchy tortilla chips and creamy avocado chunks on top. It's warmth on a cool evening; it's balm for a broken heart. It will make anyone you cook it for feel loved right down to their toes. This soup freezes well, too, so make a double batch and save some for a night when you don't feel like cooking. That's what I call loving your*self*, honey.

1 pound bone-in chicken breasts or thighs or a combination of the two

½ teaspoon salt

1 bay leaf

1 guajillo chile or 2 teaspoons chili powder

1 medium tomato, diced

1 cup diced onion (about ½ large)

3 cloves garlic, peeled

1½ teaspoons dried oregano

½ teaspoon vegetable oil

1 large zucchini, cut into thick half-circles

1½ cups sliced carrots (about 3 large)

1 cup sliced celery (about 4 large stalks)

3-4 corn tortillas, torn up

Garnish: ½ cup chopped fresh cilantro

Tortilla chips, avocado, lime wedges, and grated cheese for serving

1 Combine the chicken, 5 cups water, salt, and bay leaf in a large pot over high heat. Cover and bring to a boil. Reduce the heat to low and simmer until chicken is cooked, 15 to 20 minutes. Remove from the heat. Carefully remove the chicken with tongs and set on a cutting board to cool; set broth aside.

2 While the chicken cooks, toast the guajillo chile over a flame or a dry skillet for a few seconds. Break off the stem and shake out the seeds. (Skip this step if using chili powder.)

3 Combine the chile/chili powder, tomato, onion, ½ cup water, garlic, and oregano in a blender and puree into a smooth sauce.

4 Heat the oil in a large stockpot over medium-high heat and add the tomato sauce. It will splatter, so be careful. Cook until it turns a darker shade of red, 5 minutes. Add the zucchini, carrots, and celery and sauté 5 minutes.

5 Strain the chicken stock into the stockpot. Shred the chicken and add it, too. Cover and bring to a boil.

6 Reduce the heat to low and simmer until the vegetables are tender, 20 minutes. Add the corn tortillas and simmer a few minutes longer to thicken. Stir in cilantro.

7 Serve with any garnishes you like (but especially chips, avocado, and lime).

Note: This is a great use for leftover chicken or turkey. Instead of boiling the chicken, start with canned chicken broth and add about 2 cups of leftover shredded chicken.

KING RANCH
CHICKEN CASSEROLE

Makes 6 servings

The King Ranch is one of the oldest and biggest cattle ranches in the country, but there's no evidence that this popular chicken casserole was ever served there. It's more likely that someone co-opted the King name to make a "canned-soup-and-chicken-casserole" seem fancier—I'm betting it was the Campbell's Soup company itself. Regardless, it's comforting, it's cheap, and it's easy as hell. We ate it often when I was a kid. It's a great way to use leftover chicken or turkey (Hello, day after Thanksgiving!) and it freezes well, too. It's a perfect choice for potlucks or to bring to a family with a new baby.

1 10¾-ounce can condensed cream of chicken soup

1 10¾-ounce can condensed cream of mushroom soup

2 cups chicken broth

1 10-ounce can chopped tomatoes with green chiles, juices reserved

12 corn tortillas, quartered

3 cups diced cooked chicken or turkey

2 cups grated mild Cheddar or American cheese

1 cup diced onion

1 Heat the oven to 375°F (or use the microwave). Lightly oil a 9-by-13-inch baking dish.

2 In a large bowl, whisk together the undiluted soups, chicken broth, and canned tomatoes with juices. This is the sauce.

3 Smear the bottom of the dish with a few spoonfuls of the sauce. Now layer: ⅓ of the tortilla quarters, ½ of the chicken, ⅓ of the sauce, ⅓ of the cheese, and ½ of the onion. Repeat with the next ⅓ of the tortillas, the remaining chicken, ⅓ of the sauce, ⅓ of the cheese, and the remaining onion. Finish the top layer with the remaining tortillas, sauce, and cheese.

4 Bake until bubbling and hot, 45 minutes, or microwave on high about 10 minutes. Remove and serve hot.

CORN DOGS

Makes 8 corn dogs

Texas saw a large wave of German immigration during the 1840s. German sausage makers of the period are credited with creating the first battered and fried sausages in Texas to appeal to their new audience. Even way back then, our fondness for fried foods must have been apparent. In 1942, the Fletcher brothers introduced "Corny Dogs" at the Texas State Fair in Dallas, and what made their version different from previous fried wiener ideations was the stick. Now, fair-goers could eat Corny Dogs on the go, wherever they pleased. Next to Big Tex, corn dogs are one of the most iconic symbols of the state fair. In San Antonio, you can find a variation called a crispy dog: a cheese-stuffed hot dog wrapped in a corn tortilla and deep fried.

1 cup cornmeal

1 cup all-purpose flour

3 tablespoons granulated sugar

2 teaspoons baking powder

1½ teaspoons salt

½ cup buttermilk

½ cup ice water

4 cups shortening or peanut oil for frying

Wooden skewers or craft sticks

8 hot dogs

¼ cup cornstarch, for dredging

Mustard and ketchup for serving

1 In a large bowl, combine the cornmeal, flour, sugar, baking powder, and salt. Add the buttermilk and ice water and stir to combine (it's okay if it's a little lumpy). Set aside in the freezer or fridge while the oil heats up to 375°F (see Note for frying tips).

2 Meanwhile, skewer the hot dogs. Scatter the cornstarch in a shallow bowl and roll the hot dogs until lightly coated.

3 When the oil is hot, dip the coated hot dogs in the cold batter and fry until brown and crunchy, about 3 minutes. Remove to a paper-lined plate for 1 minute. Repeat until all the hot dogs have been fried.

4 Serve with your favorite mustard or ketchup if you're a damn maniac.

Note: I'm guessing that most of you, like me, don't have a commercial-grade deep fryer at home. I use a pot with about 3 inches of oil in it and find it's easiest to cut the hot dogs in half, making 16 shortie dogs that fit in the pot at a slant. Some people fry them horizontally in 1 inch of oil in a large skillet, rotating them to ensure they fry evenly.

CRISPY TACOS

Makes 12 tacos

As no Tex-Mex combo plate is complete without a crispy taco, no Texas cookbook is complete without a recipe for them. A crispy taco around here is universally understood to mean a crispy corn tortilla filled with simple ground beef picadillo and topped with cheese, lettuce, and hot sauce (and tomatoes and sour cream, if you're in a fancy place). In all the times I've eaten them, in homes and restaurants alike, the vast majority were made with store-bought "taco shells." So while it might seem like cheating, it *is* the real thing.

½ teaspoon oil

½ cup diced onion

1 tablespoon chili powder

½ teaspoon ground cumin

1 jalapeño pepper, minced (seeded for less heat)

2 cloves garlic, minced (2 teaspoons)

½ teaspoon crushed red pepper flakes, optional

1 pound ground beef

½ cup water, beer, or beef stock

1 teaspoon dried oregano

¼ teaspoon salt

12 crispy taco shells

Shredded cheese, lettuce, tomato, sour cream, avocado, and salsa for serving

1 Heat the oven to 150°F.

2 In a skillet over medium-high heat, warm the oil. Add the onion and sauté until translucent and slightly browned, 8 minutes. Add the chili powder and cumin and stir for 10 seconds.

3 Add the jalapeño pepper, garlic, red pepper flakes (if using), and beef. Break up the meat into chunks and then add the water. Continue to stir the meat, breaking it up as small as possible. Reduce the heat to medium and cook, stirring frequently, until the meat is no longer pink and the liquid is mostly evaporated, about 5 minutes. Add the oregano and salt and simmer another 5 minutes. Remove from the heat.

4 Place the taco shells on a baking sheet and place in the oven to warm.

5 Fill the warm taco shells with the beef picadillo and serve with the toppings of your choice.

Note: While people usually put the cheese on top, it actually works way better to put the cheese in the taco shell first and then the hot taco meat. The melted cheese creates a barrier, preventing the dreaded "crispy-taco-fall-apart" that makes young and old alike wail in frustration.

SIDES

CHARRO BEANS

Makes 8 to 12 servings (8 cups)

Charro roughly translates to "cowboy," and these are the type of beans you'll usually get at Mexican and Tex-Mex restaurants in Texas, and often at barbecue joints, too. You must use pinto beans—the mottled brown ones—but the meaty bits can be almost anything you have around. Bacon is a great start, but if you have some Mexican chorizo or leftover ham or smoked turkey wings or salt pork or even really good hot dogs, go ahead and throw those in, too. Add a bottle of dark beer at the end and you get *borracho* (drunk) beans, or mash and fry them the next day to make refried beans—three recipes in one! This will serve about 12 as a side dish, or 8 as a main dish with a slice of cornbread or a couple quesadillas on the side.

1 pound dry pinto beans

4 ounces bacon, diced

4 large cloves garlic, peeled and smashed

½ small onion, peeled but left intact

4 Roma tomatoes

3 jalapeño peppers, stems removed

½ bunch fresh cilantro, stems finely chopped and leaves separated

1 tablespoon salt

1 teaspoon freshly ground black pepper

1 bay leaf

1 12-ounce bottle dark beer, optional

1 Heat the oven to broil.

2 Sort the beans and pick out and discard anything that's not a bean or that looks shriveled and sad. Rinse the beans in a colander and set aside.

3 Get your largest pot and fry the bacon (and other meats, if using) over medium-high heat until cooked and slightly crispy. Add the beans, garlic, and 8 to 10 cups water. The beans should be covered by at least 2 inches of water. Raise the heat to high.

4 Using your broiler, roast the onion, tomatoes, and jalapeño peppers for a few minutes on each side until blistered and blackened. Seed the jalapeños if you want mild heat. Coarsely chop roasted vegetables and add to the beans with the cilantro stems, salt, black pepper, and bay leaf. Cover and bring to a boil.

5 Reduce the heat to low and crack the lid to avoid a boil-over. Simmer until tender, but not bursting, 1 to 2 hours. The cook time depends on the age of the beans; older, drier beans take longer to cook. Add more boiling water if necessary to keep the beans submerged.

6 When the beans are soft enough, you should be able to easily squish one between your thumb and finger. The beans and the bean broth should both be nice and salty. Add more salt if they need it, and simmer a few minutes longer to blend. If using beer, add it once beans are soft, then taste for salt and simmer 30 minutes uncovered to thicken and combine the flavors. Remove from the heat.

7 Stir in the cilantro leaves just before serving.

FRIED GREEN TOMATOES (OR OKRA)

Makes 2 servings

I live for the brief window of green tomato season each year. Usually around the end of summer or early fall, you can find green tomatoes at farmers' markets (or in your own garden, if you have one). These young, green tomatoes won't have time to ripen before the frost comes. While there are varieties of tomatoes that stay green even when they're ripe, that's not what you want. For fried green tomatoes to work, the tomatoes need to be firm and tart. Use this same technique to fry fresh okra.

2 to 3 green tomatoes or ½ pound okra (see Note for okra method)

½ teaspoon celery salt or seasoned salt

1 whole large egg

½ cup all-purpose flour

½ cup cornmeal

½ teaspoon salt plus more as needed

½ teaspoon freshly ground black pepper

Dash cayenne pepper, optional

2 tablespoons vegetable oil and 2 tablespoons bacon fat (or more vegetable oil) for frying

1 Slice the tomatoes to about ⅓ inch thick. Sprinkle slices with the celery salt. Beat the egg in a small bowl. In a shallow bowl, stir together the flour, cornmeal, salt, black pepper, and cayenne pepper, if using.

2 One at a time, dredge the tomato slices in the flour mixture, then the egg, and then back into the flour. Set aside on a plate or rack.

3 Once all the slices are coated, heat the oil and fat in a skillet over high heat until a bit of flour sizzles when flicked in. Carefully lay the slices in the hot skillet and reduce the heat to medium. Cook until golden on the bottom, 3 to 4 minutes. Turn and cook 3 to 4 minutes more. Remove and drain on paper or a rack. Sprinkle with a little more salt while still hot and serve right away (though these are pretty great at room temperature, too).

Note: For okra, slice into ½-inch pieces and sprinkle with celery salt. Beat the egg in a large bowl and add the okra slices. Toss around to coat. Mix the dry ingredients in another large bowl. Scoop the eggy okra out with a slotted spoon and transfer to the dry mixture. Toss around to coat. Fry the okra in a single layer, stirring occasionally, for a couple of minutes until crisp. Drain, sprinkle with more salt, and serve hot.

PERFECT POTATO SALAD

Makes 12 servings

I call this Perfect Potato Salad because it took my friends and me many trying months to perfect it for our summer cookouts. The key ingredients are celery seed and pickle juice. Use sour pickle, like dill, instead of sweet pickle juice. And while you can use waxy red potatoes, fluffy russets soak up the flavors best. This is the potato salad you want for your brisket and ribs plate, on your family reunion potluck table, and in your fridge at all times for late-night snacking over the sink.

3 pounds russet potatoes

4 stalks celery, finely chopped

4 green onions, thinly sliced

2 tablespoons minced dill pickles

¼ cup yellow mustard

2 tablespoons pickle juice

½ teaspoon celery seed

2 large hard-boiled eggs, peeled

¼ cup mayonnaise

½ teaspoon salt

½ teaspoon freshly ground black pepper

1 Boil the potatoes whole in their skins until each can be easily pierced through with a skewer, 15 to 30 minutes.

2 While the potatoes cook, chop the rest of the vegetables and place them in the bottom of a large bowl with the mustard, pickle juice, and celery seed. Set aside.

3 Transfer the boiled potatoes to an ice-water bath for 5 seconds. Slip off and discard the skins. Cut the potatoes into 1-inch chunks. Add the warm potatoes to the other vegetables in the big bowl and stir briskly. The potato chunks will break up a little, and that's what you want. Grate or mince the eggs and add those, along with the mayonnaise, salt, and black pepper, to the bowl. Stir well.

4 If it seems too dry, add more pickle juice, mustard, or mayo, depending on how you like your potato salad. Don't be afraid to taste as you go! Refrigerate at least 15 minutes to cool slightly. Will keep in the fridge up to 2 days.

Note: Sometimes I use pickled jalapeño brine instead of pickle juice. S'real good, y'all.

COLESLAW

Makes 6 servings

It's hard to say which type of slaw—mayonnaise-based or vinegar-dressed—is the most "Texas" choice. That's one of our charming regional differences. To me, mayonnaise slaw goes best with fried fish, while vinegar slaw is more often seen plated with barbecue and potato salad. The tangy vinegar cuts the richness of the barbecue. For the best texture, shred the cabbage as thinly as possible and serve the slaw within an hour of mixing it up. If you'll be making it further in advance, cut the cabbage a little thicker so it holds up better in the dressing.

¼ cup apple cider vinegar

2 tablespoons vegetable oil

1 tablespoon brown mustard

2 teaspoons granulated sugar or honey or more as needed

½ teaspoon salt or more as needed

¼ teaspoon white pepper

1 pound green cabbage, thinly shredded

1 large carrot, grated

2 green onions (green parts only), thinly sliced

1 In a large bowl, whisk together the vinegar, oil, mustard, sugar, salt, and white pepper. Add the remaining ingredients and use tongs or two forks to toss together thoroughly. By thoroughly, I mean toss your coleslaw for 1 full minute to get everything fully mixed and to make the cabbage start to wilt. Taste and add more sugar or salt as you see fit. Serve chilled.

PICKLED PEACHES

Makes 10 quarts

My family has been making these pickled peaches for at least four generations. As a kid, we had a few gnarled peach trees that produced the most exquisite white peaches, each no larger than a golf ball. They worked perfectly for this recipe. Most peaches are not small enough to fit in a canning jar, but I've used medium-sized peaches in a covered glass container rather than a jar. Eat as a side dish with beef or pork and save the syrup for adding to cocktails.

7 pounds small to medium peaches

2 ounces whole cloves

3¾ pounds granulated sugar

1 quart white vinegar

2 2-inch sticks cinnamon

1 Poke a whole clove into each peach; use 2 cloves per peach if they're medium-size.

2 Whisk together the sugar and vinegar in a large pot over high heat. Add the cinnamon sticks and cover. Bring to a boil and cook 5 minutes.

3 Carefully add the peaches and cover. Once it reaches a second boil, boil for 5 minutes. Remove from the heat. Scoop out the fruit and place in wide-mouth canning jars or a large glass storage container.

4 Boil the syrup, uncovered, another 5 minutes. Remove from the heat and pour over the fruit to cover. Seal and cool. Keep refrigerated up to 2 months.

CORNBREAD

Makes 8 servings

A proper Texas cornbread is salty and coarse, with crispy brown edges, and is baked in a cast-iron skillet. I always use whole wheat flour with the cornmeal, but you can use all-purpose white flour if you like. The result is a little less "rustic," but still good. Cornbread is best eaten hot and buttered. Serve it with Texas Chili (page 25) or Charro Beans (page 52), and for a real treat, make it for breakfast and serve coated in butter and drowned in honey. Chase that with a cold glass of buttermilk and feel like you're living in the real old-timey days.

2 tablespoons unsalted butter or bacon grease

1 cup cornmeal

1 cup whole wheat or all-purpose flour

2 teaspoons baking powder

½ teaspoon baking soda

1 whole large egg, beaten

1 cup buttermilk or thin plain yogurt

¼ cup molasses, honey, or maple syrup

1 jalapeño pepper, minced, optional

1 Heat the oven to 425°F. Put the butter or bacon fat in a 9-inch cast-iron skillet or a cake pan and put in the oven to melt the butter.

2 Whisk together the dry ingredients in a large bowl. Mix together the wet ingredients in a smaller bowl. Add the wet ingredients to the dry mixture and mix briskly—just enough to get all the dry mixture incorporated. Fold in the jalapeño pepper now, if using.

3 Carefully remove the hot skillet from the oven and pour in the batter. Bake 20 minutes. Remove from the oven; when it's ready, a toothpick inserted into the center should come out clean.

4 Cut into 8 wedges and serve.

BREAKFAST
AND
BRUNCH

BREAKFAST TACOS

Makes 4 tacos

Along with scrambled eggs, any number of things can go in a breakfast taco: potatoes, beans, bacon, sausage, cheese, *nopales* (cactus), chorizo, ham, *machacado* (dried, shredded beef), avocado, queso, or brisket, but simple is best: breakfast tacos should have three ingredients or less, and they should be made with regular-sized flour tortillas. We are not making breakfast burritos here, folks! In fact, breakfast tacos ought to be small enough to fit in a fanny pack, and most people will eat two or three in a sitting.

My personal favorite combinations are nopales and egg; chorizo and egg; potato, egg, and cheese; and bean, potato, and cheese, but there are truly endless variations. If you're overwhelmed by options, the friendly potato, egg, and cheese taco is a great starting point.

1 medium potato

¼ teaspoon ground cumin

1 tablespoon vegetable oil

Salt

Freshly ground black pepper

3 whole large eggs

1 tablespoon unsalted butter

½ cup grated Cheddar or Oaxacan cheese (or leftover queso!)

4 flour tortillas and red or green salsa for serving

1 Scrub the potato and dice into ½-inch cubes.

2 Heat the oil in a skillet over medium-high heat. Once shimmery, add the potatoes. Fry several minutes, stirring occasionally, until tender and browned. Season with the cumin, salt, and black pepper. Remove from the heat and set aside.

3 Beat the eggs with about ¼ teaspoon each of the salt and black pepper. Melt the butter in a different skillet over medium heat, add the eggs, and cook, stirring frequently, until almost set. Add the cheese and stir.

4 Warm the tortillas on a griddle or right over a gas flame. Divide the eggs and potatoes into tortillas and serve with the salsa.

Note: Breakfast tacos are gloriously portable! Before you add the salsa, wrap tacos tightly in foil and they will stay nice and warm for 1 hour or so—long enough for you to get to work and make everybody jealous with your hot, fresh tacos.

MIGAS

Makes 4 servings

Migas in Spanish means "crumbs," and this well-loved breakfast dish is likely named after the little crumbs of corn tortilla that mix in with the eggs. It was originally a way to use up stale tortillas, but most people and places nowadays just add stale tortilla chips. Either way works. I more often have tortillas on hand than I do chips, so here's how to make migas starting with corn tortillas. If you use premade chips, omit the salt in the eggs. These make a colorful plate with a side of refried beans and crispy home fries and of course are great with a hefty splatter of hot sauce all over. Or divide the migas up among four flour tortillas and make breakfast tacos.

3 corn tortillas (or 1 large handful crumbled chips)

1 tablespoon vegetable oil for frying

¼ teaspoon salt, plus more as needed

1 Roma tomato

2 tablespoons minced onion

Minced jalapeño pepper to taste

4 whole large eggs

¼ teaspoon salt

¼ teaspoon freshly ground black pepper

2 tablespoons unsalted butter

½ cup grated Cheddar or Monterey Jack

1 Stack the corn tortillas and cut into ¼-inch strips and then cut in half crosswise.

2 Warm the oil in a heavy skillet over medium-high heat and fry the strips, stirring frequently, until crispy, a few minutes. Remove from the heat, drain on paper, lightly salt, and set aside.

3 Cut the tomatoes lengthwise and gently squeeze each half to remove the seeds and liquid. Mince the tomato, onion, and jalapeño pepper.

4 In a bowl, season the eggs with the ¼ teaspoon each salt and black pepper and beat thoroughly.

5 Add 1 tablespoon butter to a skillet over medium heat. Once it melts, add the tomato, onion, and jalapeño pepper. Fry until the tomato releases its liquid and then dries out again, about 2 minutes.

6 Push to one side. Add the remaining butter to the empty half of the pan. Once it foams, add the eggs and stir until halfway set. Fold in the cooked vegetables and tortillas or chips. Sprinkle with the cheese. Cover and remove from the heat. Wait 30 seconds for the cheese to melt before serving.

KOLACHES

Makes 24 kolaches

Kolaches are a fruit pastry brought to Texas by Czech immigrants in the 1800s. The dough is rich and slightly sweet, similar to brioche, and it gets formed into little pillows upon which fruit or sweet cream cheese—or both—are piled. While a kolache (ko-LOTCH-ee) has a sweet filling, and a klobasnik has a meat filling, in Texas people tend to call them all kolaches, as in: "Two apricot kolaches, one poppy-seed kolache, and three jalapeño-sausage-cheese kolaches, please." Another thing: the proper singular form of the word is kolach, plural is kolaches, but over the years in Texas the singular has been bastardized to kolache. (We did the same thing to the tamale, for which the singular form in Spanish is really *tamal*.) This recipe for apricot kolaches comes from my great-grandmother Hornsby's collection.

FOR THE DOUGH

½ cup whole milk

2 ¼-ounce envelopes active dry yeast

12 tablespoons (1½ sticks) unsalted butter, softened

½ cup granulated sugar

1 teaspoon salt

4 large egg yolks

4½ cups sifted all-purpose flour

2 tablespoons unsalted butter, melted

FOR THE FILLING

12 ounces dried apricots or peaches

2 tablespoons granulated sugar or more as needed

¼ teaspoon freshly grated nutmeg

Make the dough:

1 Scald the milk by heating in a small pot over medium-low heat, stirring constantly, until steam rises and tiny bubbles form around the edges, a couple of minutes. Remove from the heat. Add ½ cup water and allow to cool to lukewarm (95°F to 105°F). Whisk in the yeast until dissolved and set aside.

2 In a large bowl, cream together 12 tablespoons butter, the sugar, and the salt until smooth and fluffy. Mix in the egg yolks until smooth. Add the yeast–milk mixture and 2¼ cups flour to the large bowl and beat on medium speed for 5 minutes. Add the remaining 2¼ cups flour and knead to form a firm dough. Cover and let rise in a warm place until doubled, about 1 hour.

Make the filling:

1 Finely chop the apricots and place them in a pot with the water and sugar. Simmer until softened, 10 minutes. Mash to form a chunky puree. Set aside to cool.

2 Once the dough has doubled in size, punch down and knead by hand on a floured surface for a couple of minutes. Divide into 24 balls. Arrange the balls 1 inch apart on a parchment-lined baking sheet. Brush the balls with the melted butter, cover, and let rise 45 minutes.

3 Heat the oven to 350°F.

4 Use your thumbs to make indentions in the top of each dough ball large enough to fit 2 tablespoons of the filling. Stick your thumbs into the center of each dough ball and pull outward in a circle. Fill with the apricot filling. Bake until golden brown, 12 to 15 minutes. Remove from the oven and serve warm; if not eating right away, store at room temperature and reheat for a few seconds in the microwave before serving.

BISCUITS AND GRAVY

Makes 8 biscuits with gravy

Cream gravy was one of the very first things I ever learned to make on my own. The simple recipe I still remember from back then is 2 tablespoons fat, 2 tablespoons flour, and 2 cups milk. Depending on what we had in the kitchen, the fat was either bacon fat or fat left over from frying breakfast sausage patties. When you make it with bacon fat, it's the same gravy you pour on Chicken-Fried Steak (page 32) and mashed potatoes.

FOR THE BISCUITS

1¾ cups all-purpose flour, plus more for kneading

2 teaspoons baking powder

½ teaspoon baking soda

½ teaspoon salt

6 tablespoons unsalted butter, frozen or at least very cold

¾ cup buttermilk

FOR THE GRAVY

2 tablespoons bacon or sausage fat

2 tablespoons all-purpose flour

2 cups whole or 2% milk

¾ teaspoon salt

½ teaspoon freshly ground black pepper

Make the biscuits:

1 Heat the oven to 450°F.

2 Combine the dry biscuit ingredients in a big bowl. If you thought ahead to freeze your butter, use a coarse box grater to grate it into the dry ingredients. If it's just cold, dice it small and toss it around in the mixture. Using your fingertips, mix the butter into the dry ingredients, squeezing little bits of the butter to break it up and coat it in flour. The mixture should look like pebbles. Add the buttermilk all at once and mix it up quickly.

3 Turn out the dough onto a clean, lightly floured work surface and knead by folding it over on itself several times—be gentle, as 30 seconds of kneading is plenty. Roll or pat the dough out to a ½ inch thickness. Cut with a 2-inch biscuit cutter or cut into 8 squares with a sharp knife. Place the biscuits on an ungreased cookie sheet and bake until golden, 12 to 15 minutes.

While the biscuits bake, make the gravy:

1 Warm the fat in a skillet over medium heat. Add 2 tablespoons flour and stir until lightly browned and smelling toasty, about 45 seconds. Slowly whisk in about 1 cup milk. Once a thick, smooth paste forms, whisk in the remaining 1 cup milk. Season with the salt and black pepper and taste. You will likely want more of each.

2 Split the hot biscuits open and pour gravy all over them. Serve.

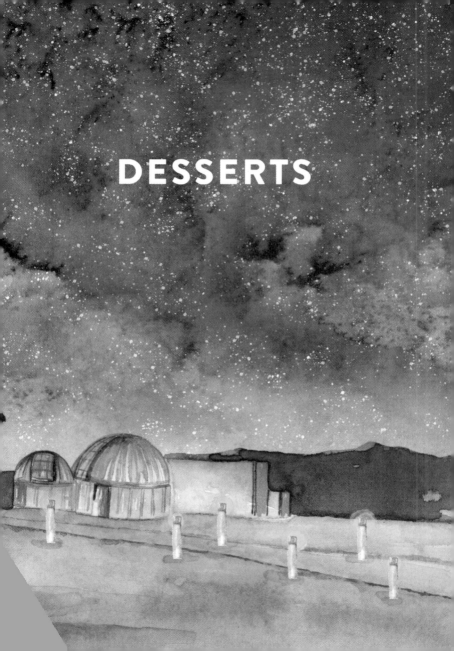

DESSERTS

PEACH COBBLER

Makes 6 servings

My mom has been making this peach cobbler since her Girl Scout days in Lometa, Texas, when she baked it in a Dutch oven over a campfire. Most cobblers have fruit on the bottom covered in a dry, biscuit-like dough, but this one puts the sugary-sweet fruit all over a simple cake batter. The result is soft and juicy, with crisp, salty edges . Use fresh peaches in summer and frozen peaches in winter. This recipe also works well with wild Texas dewberries, if you can find some

2 cups sliced peaches or whole berries	¾ cup all-purpose flour
1 cup granulated sugar	1 teaspoon baking powder
6 tablespoons salted butter	¾ cup whole or 2% milk

1 Mix the fruit with ¼ cup of the sugar and let it sit while you get the other stuff ready. If using frozen fruit, mix with the sugar while still frozen and let them sit out until thawed or microwave in short bursts on the defrost setting.

2 Heat the oven to 350°F and put the butter in an 8-inch-square baking dish. Put the dish in the oven to melt the butter.

3 In a medium bowl, whisk together the flour, remaining ¾ cup sugar, baking powder and milk—it might be lumpy, but that's okay. When the butter is melted, take the dish out (careful! it's hot!) and pour in the batter. Spoon the fruit and all accumulated juices on top. Bake until the edges are puffed and center is set, 45 to 50 minutes.

TEXAS SHEET CAKE

Makes 24 servings

A Texas sheet cake is a giant chocolate cake with a sticky chocolate-pecan icing that's served right out of the pan. It's rich and sweet and goes great with hot coffee or cold milk. This particular sheet cake recipe comes from one of my best friends, Emily, who got it from her mother, Bev. It uses a very unusual technique that makes it easy and quick to put together. The first time I made it, I didn't have enough white sugar, so I used half white and half brown sugar. I love it that way, but you may use all white sugar instead.

FOR THE CAKE

½ pound (2 sticks) unsalted butter

¼ cup cocoa powder

1 cup granulated sugar

¾ cup packed, dark brown sugar

2 cups all-purpose flour

1 teaspoon ground cinnamon

½ teaspoon salt

2 whole large eggs

½ cup buttermilk

1 teaspoon baking soda

1 teaspoon vanilla extract

FOR THE ICING

8 tablespoons (1 stick) unsalted butter

¼ cup plus 2 tablespoons whole or 2% milk

¼ cup cocoa powder

1 1-pound box confectioners' sugar

1 teaspoon vanilla extract

1 cup chopped pecans, toasted

Continued

Make the cake:

1 Heat the oven to 350°F. Grease a jelly roll or 10-by-15-inch to 13-by-18-inch sheet pan.

2 In a medium pot over medium-high heat, combine 1 cup butter, 1 cup water, and ¼ cup cocoa powder and bring to a boil. Remove from the heat and add the granulated and brown sugars. Whisk to combine.

3 In a large mixing bowl, whisk together the flour, cinnamon, and salt. Pour the contents of the pot over the dry mixture and mix well.

4 In a small bowl, beat together the eggs, buttermilk, baking soda, and 1 teaspoon vanilla. Add the contents of the small bowl to the large bowl and mix until smooth (the batter will be very thin). Pour into the greased pan and bake 20 to 25 minutes (if you use the larger pan, it requires less time). Start making the icing about 5 minutes before the cake is done.

Make the icing:

In a medium pot over medium-high heat, combine ½ cup butter, milk, and ¼ cup cocoa powder and bring to a boil. Remove from the heat and sift in the confectioners' sugar. Stir until smooth. Add 1 teaspoon vanilla and pecans and pour over the hot cake. Set aside to cool.

Note: The cake keeps well, covered, at room temperature for several days. Refrigerate for longer storage.

BOURBON PECAN PIE

Makes 1 pie

Pecan pie is a Thanksgiving staple throughout most of the United States, but it's the official state dessert of Texas. Most pecan pies are light on the pecan and heavy on the corn syrup, resulting in a cloyingly sweet pie that lacks the wonderful nuttiness of pecans. This recipe from my great-grandmother Hornsby is chock full of pecans. Toasting the nuts before adding them to the pie boosts their flavor and turns out a sophisticated pie. Serve with softly whipped cream.

3 whole large eggs

1 cup granulated sugar

1 cup dark Karo syrup

2 tablespoons bourbon or 1 teaspoon vanilla extract

2 tablespoons unsalted butter

2 cups coarsely chopped pecans

1 deep-dish 9-inch piecrust

Softly whipped cream for serving

1 Heat the oven to 375°F.

2 In a large bowl, whisk together the eggs, sugar, Karo syrup, and bourbon. Set aside.

3 In a skillet over medium heat, melt the butter. Add the pecans and toast until they start to smell nutty, about 3 minutes. Add to the egg mixture and stir together. Pour into the piecrust.

4 Bake until the pie is slightly puffed but the center is still a little jiggly, 35 to 45 minutes. Remove from the oven and cool completely. Serve cold or at room temperature.

BANANA PUDDING

Makes 6 servings

Banana pudding is great to make ahead of time, as it holds up in the fridge. As it chills, the banana flavor infuses the pudding and the cookies swell up into tiny, soft cakes. Top it with more crunchy cookies before serving to get a nice textural contrast.

⅓ cup granulated sugar

2 tablespoons cornstarch

2 cups cold whole or 2% milk

2 large egg yolks

2 tablespoons unsalted
butter, cut into bits

1 teaspoon vanilla extract

1 large ripe banana,
peeled and sliced

30 vanilla wafer cookies,
plus more for serving

1 In a medium pot, whisk together the sugar, cornstarch, and milk until the sugar and cornstarch are dissolved. Add the egg yolks and whisk again. Add the butter and place the pot over medium heat.

2 Stir constantly until the mixture just begins to bubble, about 5 minutes. Reduce the heat to low and simmer, stirring constantly, 2 minutes more, until thickened. Do not overcook, as overcooking will "break" it, and it won't set up. Remove from the heat and stir in the vanilla. Set aside.

3 Layer ½ the cookies and ½ the banana slices in the bottom of a 1½-quart dish. Top with ½ the pudding, the remaining banana slices, cookies, and pudding. Top with more cookies or lay a piece of plastic wrap right over the top of the pudding and refrigerate 4 to 8 hours.

4 Add more crispy cookies and serve.

ACKNOWLEDGMENTS

Everything I know about Texas cooking, I learned
through years spent in the kitchen and around the
dining table with my parents and grandmothers.
Without their time and teaching, I could not have
written this book. Endless gratitude also goes to my
husband, Chris, who has encouraged my writing
and been my best advocate since the day we met. And
thanks to my darling agent, Martha, who emailed me
one day on a hunch.

Courtney Jentzen would like to thank Carly Martin for
her help with the illustrations. Thanks also to Redding,
Stevie, and Paul.

INDEX